May 2016

MARTIN LUTHER KING JR.
AND THE MARCH ON WASHINGTON

by Stephanie Watson

Content Consultant
Michael Honey
Professor of Humanities
University of Washington, Tacoma

Core Library

abdopublishing.com

Published by Abdo Publishing, a division of ABDO, PO Box 398166, Minneapolis, Minnesota 55439. Copyright © 2016 by Abdo Consulting Group, Inc. International copyrights reserved in all countries. No part of this book may be reproduced in any form without written permission from the publisher. Core Library™ is a trademark and logo of Abdo Publishing.

Printed in the United States of America, North Mankato, Minnesota

052015
092015

Cover Photo: AP Images/© 1963 Dr. Martin Luther King, Jr. © renewed 1991 Coretta Scott King
Interior Photos: AP Images/© 1963 Dr. Martin Luther King, Jr. © renewed 1991 Coretta Scott King, 1; AP Images, 4, 17, 19, 28, 31, 32, 36, 40, 43, 45; Warren K. Leffler/Library of Congress, 7; AP Images/© 1963 Dr. Martin Luther King, Jr. © renewed 1991 Coretta Scott King, 10; Marion Post Wolcott/Library of Congress, 12; Bill Hudson/AP Images, 20; New York World-Telegram and the Sun Newspaper Photograph Collection/Library of Congress, 22; Abbie Rowe/National Park Service, 25; AP Images/© 1964 Dr. Martin Luther King, Jr. © renewed 1992 Coretta Scott King, 39; I Have a Dream speech/© 1963 Dr. Martin Luther King, Jr. © renewed 1991 Coretta Scott King, 41

Editor: Mirella Miller
Series Designer: Becky Daum

Library of Congress Control Number: 2015931189

Cataloging-in-Publication Data
Watson, Stephanie.
 Martin Luther King Jr. and the March on Washington / Stephanie Watson.
  p. cm. -- (Stories of the civil rights movement)
Includes bibliographical references and index.
ISBN 978-1-62403-881-5
1. March on Washington for Jobs and Freedom (1963: Washington, D.C.)--Juvenile literature. 2. African Americans--Civil rights--History--20th century--Juvenile literature. 3. Civil rights movements--United States--History--20th century--Juvenile literature.   I. Title.
323.1196--dc23
                                                      2015931189

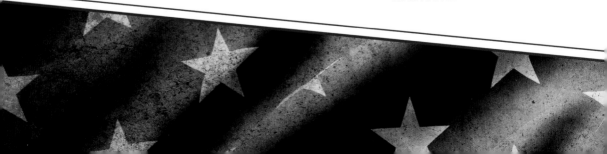

CONTENTS

I HAVE A DREAM

The afternoon of August 28, 1963, was hot and sticky in Washington, DC. More than 250,000 people packed the National Mall. They filled the area between the Washington Monument and the Lincoln Memorial. Some people fanned themselves to cool off. Others dipped their toes in the waters of the Reflecting Pool.

Thousands of people packed the National Mall on August 28, 1963.

These people had come to Washington, DC, from almost every state in the nation. They were a mix of cultures, ages, and religions. Some people were African American; others were white. They were young and old, and came from different religious backgrounds. All of them had come to take part in the March on Washington for Jobs and Freedom.

Civil Rights and the Lincoln Memorial

The Lincoln Memorial was built as a tribute to Abraham Lincoln's belief in freedom for all people—regardless of their skin color. It became an important site of the civil rights movement. In 1939 singer Marian Anderson performed there when she was not allowed to sing at Constitution Hall in Washington, DC, because she was African American. The 1957 Prayer Pilgrimage and 1963 March on Washington were also held at the Lincoln Memorial.

Leading up to the March

One hundred years had passed since President Abraham Lincoln signed the Emancipation Proclamation, freeing some African Americans from slavery. However,

Even taxis in the South were not equal. Some taxis were listed as "White Only."

in 1963, African Americans were free, but not equal. In the South, they could not eat at the same lunch counters or go to the same schools as white people. All across the country, they earned less money than whites in the same jobs.

African Americans were tired of being treated unfairly. In the summer of 1963, they fought back with peaceful protests throughout the South. They held sit-ins, where they sat at lunch counters that usually would not serve them. African Americans refused to ride buses where they were forced to sit in the back.

And they marched with signs asking for equal rights. These small acts turned into a movement. It was called the civil rights movement.

Protest was not easy. White police attacked the protesters with water hoses and dogs. Some protesters were beaten. Bombs were thrown at their homes and churches. Yet still the protesters pressed on.

August 28, 1963

Earlier on this hot summer day, thousands of people had marched through the streets of Washington, DC. Then they filed into the area in front of the Lincoln Memorial. They listened as civil rights leaders gave speeches calling for justice. They wanted dignity and equality for people of all races.

Finally only one speaker was left. He was a 34-year-old pastor from Atlanta, Georgia. Over the last few years, he had established himself as a leader of the civil rights movement. He had led the 1955 bus boycott in Montgomery, Alabama, and had joined sit-ins in Birmingham, Alabama. For his efforts, he was attacked, arrested, and thrown in jail.

The crowd had waited all day to hear this one man. Martin Luther King Jr. made his way to the podium. Below him the people cheered and clapped. King raised his arm to them in greeting. Then he spoke slowly, in a deep, rich voice. "I am happy to join with you today in what will go down in history as the greatest demonstration for freedom in the history of our nation," he began.

For the next 16 minutes, King spoke of his dream. He dreamed of a day when all Americans

Martin Luther King Jr.

Martin Luther King Jr. was born on January 15, 1929, in Atlanta, Georgia. His father, the Reverend Martin Luther King Sr., was a pastor at Ebenezer Baptist Church. King wanted to become a preacher too. He studied at Crozer Theological Seminary. At age 18, he was ordained a minister. King was a good speaker. He knew how to move people with his words. One of his parishioners said, "When I hears [sic] Dr. King, I see angel's wings flying 'round his head."

King's "I Have a Dream" speech would become one of the most famous speeches in US history.

were equal. He dreamed of a country where his children would be judged by the people they were inside—not by the color of their skin. Over and over, he said the words, "I have a dream." Across the National Mall and all over the United States people listened. They cheered and they cried.

On that August day in 1963, African Americans were about to change their destiny. It was their time. The March on Washington was their moment. And Martin Luther King Jr. was their voice.

EXPLORE ONLINE

The focus in Chapter One is on civil rights and the March on Washington. The website below also focuses on the March on Washington. As you know, every source is different. How is the information given in the website different from the information in this chapter? What information is the same? How do the two sources present information differently? What can you learn from this website?

March on Washington: Special Collection
mycorelibrary.com/march-on-washington

CHAPTER TWO

LIBERTY FOR SOME

The 1950s and 1960s were not easy times for African Americans. Approximately 12 million of the country's 19 million African-American residents lived in the South under Jim Crow laws. These laws kept African Americans separate from whites. African Americans could not use the same public bathrooms or drinking fountains as white people. They had to stay in separate hotels. They

In many areas of the South, African Americans could not use the same movie theaters as white people.

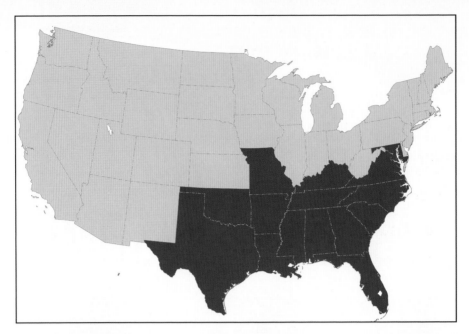

Jim Crow Laws

This map shows the states that had Jim Crow laws in place for public areas. These laws forced African Americans to use separate libraries, restaurants, parks, and other public spaces. What does this map tell you about the rights of African Americans under Jim Crow laws? How does it help you better understand the civil rights movement?

could only use their own beaches and restaurants. This was called segregation.

Bus Boycott

African Americans in the South were forced to sit in the back of buses. They also had to give up their seat if a white person wanted it. On December 1, 1955, a seamstress named Rosa Parks refused to give up her seat to a white man on a Birmingham bus. It was a simple act of defiance. But Parks's refusal sparked other African Americans to also say they were tired of giving in.

On December 5, 1955, a group called the Montgomery Improvement Association (MIA) formed. It was made up of local African-American leaders and ministers. Martin Luther King Jr. became its leader. In his first speech to the MIA, he said, " . . . there comes a time

CIVIL RIGHTS VOICES
Rosa Parks

. . . I felt that I had a right to be treated as any other passenger. We had endured that kind of treatment for too long.

On December 1, 1955, Rosa Parks took a Montgomery city bus home. She worked as a seamstress at a department store. She was tired and her feet hurt. She sat in the back of the bus. A white man came on the crowded bus. The bus driver demanded Parks give up her seat. But on this day, she refused and was arrested. Her simple act of defiance sparked the Montgomery Bus Boycott and helped launch the civil rights movement.

when people get tired of being trampled over by the iron feet of oppression."

To protest segregation on Montgomery's buses, the group planned a boycott. African Americans stopped riding buses to work and school. They walked and created a carpool group instead. The boycott lasted 381 days. In December 1956, the US Supreme Court desegregated Montgomery city buses. No longer would African-American people be forced to the back of the bus.

A Movement Begins

King and civil rights groups had achieved a real victory for African Americans in Montgomery. He wanted to do the same for all African Americans in the United States. In 1957 King helped start the Southern Christian Leadership Conference (SCLC). Its goal was to end segregation and discrimination against African Americans. Unlike a few other groups working for African-American rights, King wanted to use peaceful protest—not violence—to achieve these goals.

After the boycott ended, African Americans could sit in any seat they wanted.

King spoke about civil rights around the country. On May 17, 1957, he led the Prayer Pilgrimage at the Lincoln Memorial in Washington, DC. During the pilgrimage, he and other civil rights leaders spoke to a crowd of approximately 25,000 demonstrators. They urged the federal government to fulfill the promise of *Brown v. Board of Education*, a case the Supreme

Court had decided three years earlier. This decision outlawed segregation in schools. But most states still had separate schools for African-American and white children. The Prayer Pilgrimage was the largest civil rights gathering up to that time.

By 1960 the civil rights movement was taking hold across the South. African-American college students held sit-ins at restaurants that would not otherwise serve them. Groups of civil rights activists rode buses through the South to protest segregated bus stations. These were called Freedom Rides.

Sit-ins

On February 1, 1960, four African-American college students sat down at a whites-only lunch counter in a department store in Greensboro, North Carolina. The students were not served. They were harassed and attacked. Instead of leaving, they sat still to protest the unequal treatment of African Americans. This was the very first organized sit-in. Many other sit-ins followed across the South. The sit-in became one of the most powerful kinds of protest in the civil rights movement.

An African-American teenager participates in a sit-in at a lunch counter in Birmingham.

Birmingham Dogs

In the spring of 1963, civil rights activists launched a series of protests in Birmingham, called the Birmingham Campaign. Crowds of people peacefully marched through the streets of the city. They walked arm in arm, singing "We Shall Overcome," a protest song that became the anthem of the civil rights movement.

19

Birmingham police used attack dogs to make the crowd disperse.

Police sprayed the peaceful protesters with fire hoses. Many of the protesters were children as young as six years old. People around the country saw the protests on TV. Many of them were outraged at the way African Americans were being treated. President

John F. Kennedy saw film of a police dog lunging at an African-American woman. He was sickened by the actions. He sent troops to Birmingham. On May 10, 1963, the city desegregated its lunch counters, bathrooms, and drinking fountains. It was another big win for civil rights, but African Americans still had a long way to go to achieve equality.

FURTHER EVIDENCE

Chapter Two covers the Montgomery Bus Boycott, the Birmingham Campaign, and the start of the civil rights movement. What was one of the chapter's main points? What are some pieces of evidence in the chapter that support this main point? Check out the website at the link below. Does the information on this website support the main point in this chapter? Write a few sentences using new information from the website as evidence to support the main point in this chapter.

Civil Rights Movement
mycorelibrary.com/march-on-washington

CHAPTER THREE

PLANNING A MASSIVE MARCH

Martin Luther King Jr. knew the civil rights movement was on the verge of a breakthrough. He also knew the greatest weapon the movement had was peaceful protest. But what should they do next?

Civil rights leader A. Philip Randolph had an idea. He wanted to stage a mass march on Washington, DC. Thousands of people would gather in the nation's

A. Philip Randolph was a key leader in starting the March on Washington.

A. Philip Randolph

A community is democratic only when the humblest and weakest person can enjoy the highest civil, economic, and social rights that the biggest and most powerful possess.

A. Philip Randolph began fighting for African-American rights during World War I (1914–1918). In 1925 he formed the first African-American union. Randolph told President Franklin D. Roosevelt in 1941 that he was going to stage a march in Washington for more African-American jobs. Randolph never got the chance. In June 1941, President Roosevelt signed an executive order to make certain kinds of job discrimination illegal.

capital. There they would demand equal job opportunities, voting, and civil rights laws to ensure equality.

In the spring of 1963, Randolph and another civil rights leader, Bayard Rustin, began to plan the march. It would be called the March on Washington for Jobs and Freedom. King did not help plan the march. But he would give a speech that day to inspire the crowd.

President Kennedy Steps In

On June 11, 1963, President Kennedy gave

Kennedy's speech promised social and economic equality for African Americans.

a speech on television. He told the country he was submitting a new civil rights bill to Congress. The bill was part of Kennedy's effort to fulfill the promise of equality he had made to African Americans when he was elected president in 1960. It was a promise Abraham Lincoln had started when he signed the Emancipation Proclamation 100 years before. The speech gave civil rights activists new hope. But then there was a setback.

On June 12, a Ku Klux Klan member shot and killed civil rights activist Medgar Evers in front of his Mississippi home. The Klan was a racist group

Medgar Evers

Civil rights leader Medgar Evers was born in Mississippi in 1925. Evers served in World War II (1939–1945). In the early 1950s, he joined the civil rights movement. He became president of a Mississippi civil rights group. In 1954 he was chosen as the first field officer of the National Association for the Advancement of Colored People's Mississippi office. Evers led boycotts against white businesses that would not serve African Americans. On June 12, 1963, a Klan member shot and killed Evers. He was buried at Arlington National Cemetery in Virginia with full military honors.

that terrorized African Americans. His death led to huge protests around the country. More than 100,000 people joined those protests. President Kennedy urged the nation to keep calm.

On June 22, President Kennedy called King and the other March on Washington leaders to the White House. He asked them to postpone the march. He wanted to give Congress time to pass the civil rights bill. Randolph and King said the march had to go on. The president reluctantly gave his approval. A date was set: August 28, 1963.

On the evening of June 11, 1963, President John F. Kennedy went on television to speak to the nation. During his famous speech, he called on Americans to support civil rights and equal treatment for African Americans:

> One hundred years of delay have passed since President Lincoln freed the slaves. Yet their heirs, their grandsons are not fully free. They are not yet free from the bonds of injustice. They are not yet free from social and economic oppression. And this nation, for all its hopes and all its boasts, will not be fully free until all its citizens are free.
>
> Source: "From the Archives: JFK Address on Civil Rights." NBC Nightly News. NBC News.com, 2014. Web. Accessed December 10, 2014.

What's the Big Idea?

Take a close look at this speech. What is President Kennedy trying to say about the rights of African Americans? Pick out two details he uses to make his point. What does he mean when he says "bonds of injustice"?

CHAPTER FOUR

A FORCE OF NATURE

On August 28, 1963, dawn broke on a still-sleeping Washington, DC. But across the country, people were moving. Buses, trains, and cars were on their way to Washington, DC, from all over the country. One group of marchers even walked all the way from Brooklyn, New York. They traveled more than 200 miles (322 km) on foot.

Hundreds of people gather in Wilmington, North Carolina, to board buses to Washington, DC.

The first bus to arrive in the city brought 38 students from Mississippi. They walked off the bus singing freedom songs, which had become songs of the civil rights movement. The first Freedom Train pulled into Union Station at 8:02 a.m. It had been chartered to bring members of the civil rights movement to Washington. The train carried 535 passengers. As the marchers arrived from all over the country, people who lived in Washington, DC, came out of their homes to

People sat on the National Mall's lawn relaxing or eating lunch while waiting for the march to begin.

wave and greet them. Not everyone was in favor of the march, though. Approximately 70 members of the racist American Nazi party showed up to protest. Police quickly surrounded them to keep the peace.

By 9:30 a.m., nearly 23,000 people had gathered at the Washington Monument. Nearly two hours later, 90,000 people of all ages and races had arrived. Folk singers Joan Baez , Bob Dylan, Mahalia Jackson, and Peter, Paul, and Mary entertained the crowd. The Student Nonviolent Coordinating Committee (SNCC) Freedom Singers from Georgia also performed.

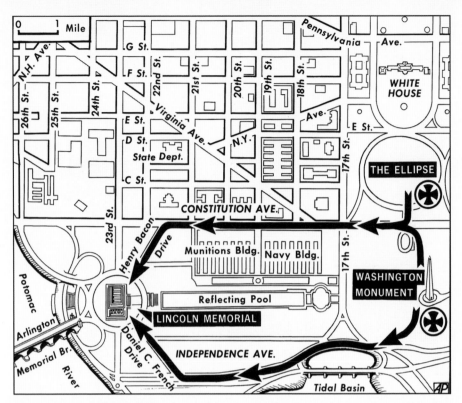

The March Route

The marchers assembled at the Washington Monument on the far end of the National Mall. Then they fanned out in two directions. Some walked down Constitution Avenue. Others walked down Independence Avenue. They met at the Lincoln Memorial for the speeches. Why do you think the protestors chose this route?

First Steps

The march began just after 11:00 a.m. There were two

march routes. Some people walked down Constitution

Avenue. Others walked down Independence Avenue.

They filled the streets. Martin Luther King Jr. and

other march leaders linked arms and held hands as they walked. Some of the marchers carried signs that read, "We demand voting rights now!" and "We march for minimum wage coverage for all workers now!"

The marchers spread out on both sides of the Reflecting Pool and up the steps of the Lincoln Memorial. Leaders took their places in front of the Memorial, in the shadow of the great Abraham Lincoln statue. Rosa Parks and other famous members of the civil rights movement sat on the stage. Joining them were some other famous faces. Actors Charlton Heston, Marlon Brando, Rita Moreno, and Sidney Poitier, as well as singer Harry Belafonte, came to show their support. Below them the crowd had swelled to 250,000 people. Millions more people watched the event on television or listened in on the radio.

Messages of Hope

Opera singer Camilla Williams started the program by singing "The Star-Spangled Banner." Then each

CIVIL RIGHTS VOICES
John Lewis

To those who have said, be patient and wait, we must say that we cannot be patient, we do not want our freedom gradually but we want to be free now!

John Lewis was a leader of the civil rights movement. He was inspired to join the movement after he heard Martin Luther King Jr. speak on the radio. Lewis led sit-ins and took part in Freedom Rides. In the early 1960s, he helped form the Student Nonviolent Coordinating Committee (SNCC). At just 23 years old, he was one of the main speakers at the March on Washington. By 2015, Lewis was serving his 14th term as a US Congressman from Georgia.

speaker stepped up to the podium. Randolph promised they would carry the civil rights movement to every part of the country. SNCC chairman John Lewis told the audience they could no longer be patient and wait for equal rights. One by one, other leaders of the march spoke to the crowd.

At around 3:00 p.m., gospel singer Mahalia Jackson performed the spiritual, "I Been 'Buked and I Been Scorned." Then the moment everyone had been waiting for finally arrived. A. Philip Randolph came to the podium to announce the featured speaker, Dr. Martin Luther King Jr.

The crowd cheered and chanted King's name as he stepped up to the microphone. After the noise quieted down, he began to speak. He spoke slowly and with great feeling. Sometimes he would draw out a vowel sound very long. At other times, he would repeat words or pause for emphasis. Every word and pause was filled with meaning.

King spoke of the promise made in the Declaration of Independence that "black men as well as white men, would be guaranteed the unalienable rights of life, liberty, and the pursuit of happiness." That promise had not yet been granted. He spoke of a dream that, in segregated states, such as Alabama, children of all races would be able to hold hands and be friends.

As King spoke of his dream, his voice built in emotion. It built until he shouted out his final words,

People cheered, hugged, and wept after King finished his famous speech.

taken from an old song: "Free at last, free at last, thank God almighty, we are free at last!"

Civil rights activist James Farmer said King's "I Have a Dream" speech would go down as one of the most important speeches in US history. Farmer said that, in that moment, King was touched by the kind of spirit that would never occur again in his lifetime.

After the March

The March on Washington was a proud moment in the civil rights movement. It gave African Americans all over the United States a new sense of hope. Lerone Bennett Jr., editor of *Ebony* magazine, called it a force of nature. President Kennedy said the country could be proud of the March on Washington. The march also proved King's place as leader of the civil rights movement. *Time* magazine named him its "Man of the Year" in 1963. In 1964 he won the Nobel Peace Prize.

But the March on Washington did not fully heal the country. On September 15, 1963, the Klan bombed Birmingham's Sixteenth Street Baptist Church. Four African-American girls were killed. On November 22, President Kennedy was assassinated in Dallas, Texas. He had not yet had a chance to sign his civil rights bill into law.

Kennedy's successor, President Lyndon B. Johnson, signed the Civil Rights Act of 1964 on

July 2, 1964. King was there to witness the signing. The act banned segregation in public places, such as buses, restaurants, and swimming pools. Soon after came the Voting Rights Act of 1965, which made sure every African American had the right to vote. Some people believe the March on Washington helped to get these acts signed.

King's Last Words

On April 3, 1968, Martin Luther King Jr. gave a speech at the Mason Temple in Memphis, Tennessee. He talked about how much the civil rights movement had already accomplished—and how much more it would achieve. He said he had been to the top of the mountain and had seen the Promised Land. Though he was not sure if he would get there with his followers, he promised them they all would one day get to the Promised Land, which meant freedom and equality.

The very next day, King was standing on his balcony at the Lorraine Motel in Memphis when

President Johnson shakes hands with King after signing the Civil Rights Act of 1964.

James Earl Ray shot him. He died one hour later. President Johnson told the country that an empty space had been left when King was killed. President Johnson believed that King's dream had not died with him.

Johnson was right—King's dream did not die with him. But it did face some setbacks along the way. Discrimination did not disappear overnight. But

African Americans slowly had more rights and could use the same public spaces as white people, including attending the same schools.

African Americans began to have more opportunities. They could go to the college of their choice and have the type of career they wanted. They could eat, sit, and play wherever they chose.

The March on Washington and King's "I Have a Dream" speech are now considered landmark moments in the civil rights movement. They symbolize a movement that continues to fight for progress, change, and freedom for all.

Martin Luther King Jr. delivered his most famous speech in the shadow of the Lincoln Memorial, at the end of the March on Washington:

> *I have a dream that one day this nation will rise up and live out the true meaning of its creed, "We hold these truths to be self-evident, that all men are created equal." I have a dream that one day on the red hills of Georgia, sons of former slaves and the sons of former slave owners will be able to sit down together at the table of brotherhood. . . . I have a dream that my four little children will one day live in a nation where they will not be judged by the color of their skin, but by the content of their character. I have a dream today!*
>
> Source: Martin Luther King Jr. "I Have a Dream." The King Center. *The King Center,* 2014. Web. Accessed January 13, 2015.

Consider Your Audience

Review this passage closely. Consider how you would adapt it for a different audience, such as your classmates. Write an article describing this same information for the new audience. How is your new approach different from the original text and why?

SNAPSHOT OF MARTIN LUTHER KING JR.'S SPEECH

Martin Luther King Jr. stands on a stage in front of the Lincoln Memorial. He waves to the 250,000 people who have gathered on the National Mall for the March on Washington.

Date
August 28, 1963

Key Players
Martin Luther King Jr., A. Philip Randolph, Bayard Rustin, John Lewis, John F. Kennedy

What Happened
On August 28, 1963, 250,000 Americans of all ages, races, and religions took part in the March on Washington for Jobs and Freedom. After marching through the streets of Washington, DC, they gathered in front of the Lincoln Memorial. Their goal was an end to segregation. They wanted African Americans to have equal rights in jobs, at school, and in all public places.

Impact

The March on Washington was a landmark moment in the civil rights movement. It publicized the need for equality in the United States. The march and Martin Luther King Jr.'s "I Have a Dream" speech became symbols of the movement. On July 2, 1964, President Lyndon Johnson signed the Civil Rights Act of 1964. The act banned segregation in public places such as buses, restaurants, and swimming pools.

Take a Stand

This book discusses why President Kennedy wanted Martin Luther King Jr. and other leaders to postpone the march. Do you think they should have postponed the march as the president asked them to do? Or should they have kept the march on schedule, as they did? Write a short essay explaining your opinion. Make sure to give reasons for your opinion, and facts and details that support those reasons.

You Are There

This book discusses the nonviolent tactics civil rights activists used to push for change, such as sit-ins and marches. Imagine you are an African-American student living in the South in the 1960s. Would you take part in a sit-in, even though you know you might be beaten or arrested? Do you think your friends would take part in these civil rights protests? How would your parents feel about it if you participated?

Say What?

Studying the civil rights movement can mean learning a lot of new vocabulary. Find five words in this book that you've never heard before. Use a dictionary to find out what they mean. Then write the meanings in your own words, and use each word in a new sentence.

Why Do I Care?

The March on Washington happened more than 50 years ago. But its goals are still important today. How might life be different for you or your friends if the march had never happened? Use your imagination!

GLOSSARY

activists
people who protest or push for social change

bill
a draft of a law that is given to the US Congress to be passed

boycott
to avoid buying, using, or doing something in protest

desegregated
ending a policy denying people access to a place or service because of their race, age, or other factors

discrimination
to deny people the right to do something or be somewhere because of their race, age, or other factors

emancipation
setting someone free

oppression
unjust or unfair treatment

protester
someone who expresses his or her feeling that an action or law is unfair

segregation
a policy that forces people to be separate because of their race or other factors

union
a group of workers who join together to protect their rights at work

LEARN MORE

Books

Bader, Bonnie. *Who Was Martin Luther King, Jr.?* New York: Grosset & Dunlap, 2008.

Kenney, Karen Latchana. *Rosa Parks and the Montgomery Bus Boycott.* Minneapolis: Abdo Publishing, 2015.

Krull, Kathleen. *What Was the March on Washington?* New York: Grosset & Dunlap, 2013.

Websites

To learn more about Stories of the Civil Rights Movement, visit **booklinks.abdopublishing.com.** These links are routinely monitored and updated to provide the most current information available.

Visit **mycorelibrary.com** for free additional tools for teachers and students.

INDEX

ABOUT THE AUTHOR

Stephanie Watson is a freelance writer and editor based in Rhode Island. Over her 20-plus-year career, she has written for television, radio, the Web, and print. Watson has authored more than 24 books.